Inspiring stories of faith, hope and tr̶a̶
world. These stories are like windows ┊
worlds: each of them has a specific co̶n̶t̶e̶x̶t̶ ̶a̶n̶d̶ ̶o̶t̶h̶e̶r̶
them with their own struggles and hopes. Although these stories are
very different in many aspects, they have two things in common: the
recognition of God's divine touch, in very concrete and unique ways,
and the engagement of local churches in the transformation of their
reality. Readers will be captivated by Richard's thoughtful reflections
around theology, discipleship and social action, in warm and
compelling ways.

> *Maria Andrade, Theology and Network Engagement Global Lead,*
> *Tearfund (Ecuador)*

This book inspired me to continue to work to bring transformation in
my own context. I hope it will be a great blessing and give life and
motivation to thousands across the world.

> *VL (India)*

Really helpful. It's a great read, making the theology understandable
and with stories that really highlight what God is doing through his
church around the world. I was already joining the dots in my mind
about what churches here in the minority world could learn.

> *Diane Holt, Thrive Ireland Director (UK)*

This is a book that invites us to rethink about our life purposes and the
mission of God's church.

> *Dr Raymond Kwong, Tearfund Country Director*
> *East and South-East Asia (China)*

This book an important and revelatory focus on the potential for fuller
lives for all in church and community – when those who know Jesus,
also show Jesus and share Jesus! This is a book well worth reading,
sharing and studying.

> *Rev David Brown, Church of Ireland Minister (UK)*

It's a great book! Your writing style is very attractive and readable, and
I love all the stories throughout.

> *Rev Ian Hughes (England)*

I recommend that Christians read this easily readable book and discuss it in groups to discover how their communities can flourish. With its theological perspectives, the book would also be suitable for use in theological institutions.

Rev Dr Sas Conradie, Tearfund Theology and Network Engagement Manager, Africa (South Africa / UK)

Communicates a stirring passion towards practical and meaningful engagements in communities. Such passion can have a lasting impact when initiatives are done in the light of God's vision of restoration, with all of God's people, and out of trust in God's transformative power.

Pastor Sur Del Rosario, ICI Ministries Foundation Department Head (Philippines)

The book is an excellent and informative guide complete with inspiring stories for those of us who appreciate life in God's field. It is timely and a must-read, which I recommend to anyone whose raison d'être is to bring hope to those for whom hope is in short supply.

Dr Barnabé Anuruni Msabah, Tearfund East and Central Africa CCT Coordinator and Research Associate, University of Stellenbosch and author of The Wayfarer *(DRC/ Kenya)*

You'll not find a more welcoming and stimulating invitation to church and community transformation!

Professor Monty Lynn, Abilene Christian University and co-author of Development in Mission (USA)

I am really impressed by the level of connection with real life. Every story and example encourages us to live out faith in a very practical way.

Romnal Colas, Tearfund Latin America and the Caribbean Church and Community Transformation Lead (Haiti)

FLOURISH

FULLER LIFE FOR ALL THROUGH CHURCH AND COMMUNITY TRANSFORMATION

Regnum Series Preface

While we delight to serve the academic community, our mission is to enable the global church to engage more readily in God's mission in its very diverse contexts. To do this we seek to bring practitioners and academics together. Our desire is that this series will bridge the gap that sometimes exists between, on the one hand, Christian leaders and mission practitioners and, on the other, Christian researchers.

About the Author

Richard Lister's heart is to see *the whole world filled with the knowledge of the glory of the LORD as the waters cover the sea* (Habakkuk 2 v14). He has over 20 years of experience in helping churches and communities to bring transformation in Asia, Africa, South America, Europe and North America. Richard works as a Church and Community Transformation Specialist for Tearfund and as a leadership mentor and coach for Coaching to Thrive (coachingtothrive.org).

FLOURISH

FULLER LIFE FOR ALL THROUGH CHURCH AND COMMUNITY TRANSFORMATION

Richard Lister

Copyright © Richard Lister 2022

First published 2022 by Regnum Books International
in association with Redcliffe College

Regnum is an imprint of the Oxford Centre for Mission Studies
St. Philip and St. James Church, Woodstock Road, Oxford, OX2 6HR, UK
www.regnumbooks.net

09 08 07 06 05 04 03 8 7 6 5 4 3 2 1

The right of Richard Lister to be identified as the author of this work
has been asserted by him in accordance with the Copyright, Designs
and Patents Act 1988.

British Library Cataloguing in Publication Data
A catalogue record for this book is available from the British Library

ISBN: 978-1-914454-53-0

Typeset in Palatino by WORDS BY DESIGN
Printed and bound in Great Britain

Cover image Tom Price / Tearfund

regnum

'For the earth will be filled with the knowledge of the glory of the LORD, as the waters cover the sea'
Habakkuk 2:14

'Just follow Jesus. Keep following the great big God rather than focusing too much on the great big vision'
Arthur Thangai, Mumbai Transformation Network

'I have come that they may have life, life in all its fullness'
John 10:10

DEDICATION

To all the young people, women and men who courageously work to help transform their communities and nations. You are an inspiration.

CONTENTS

Terms Explained   xi

1. It Doesn't Work   1

God's Vision

2. Where Is Life?   9

3. Shrunken Gospel and Sleeping Giant   13

4. If We Are True Believers,
   Then Why Are We Killing Each Other?   21

All God's People

5. Football with Blinkers   31

6. We Can't Change the World   37

7. Five Loaves and Two Fish   44

8. My Money Is in the World   51

9. The Same Calling   57

Our God

10. And Imagine If ...   67

Appendix 1: Principles   73

Appendix 2: Life in All Its Fullness 'Ecosystem'   75

Acknowledgements   77

Church and Community Transformation (CCT)	Involves local churches working with their communities to bring improvements in every area of life.
Discipleship	'Discipleship is a calling to be active collaborators with God for the transforming of the world' and 'Discipleship is a total God-ward transformation.'[1]
Kingdom of God (or kingdom of heaven)	The kingdom of God is where God is ruling over his people. It is characterised by life in all its fullness and dynamic, wholesome relationships (*shalom* in Hebrew). The heart of Jesus' teaching centres around the kingdom of God throughout Matthew, Mark and Luke.[2]
Integral mission	'The task of bringing the whole of life under the lordship of Jesus Christ and includes the affirmation that there is no biblical dichotomy between evangelistic and social responsibility in bringing Christ's peace to the poor and oppressed.'[3]

---

[1] Both quoted in 'Laying a Firm Foundation', Tim Raby, Consultancy Report for Tearfund, April 2019.
[2] Biblestudytools.com
[3] https://lausanne.org/networks/issues/integral-mission

Majority World	Often called 'developing countries, third world or global south'. However, Majority World makes clear that the vast majority of people live in these economically poorer countries. The UN predicts that, by 2030, 85% of the world's population will live in these parts of the world.[4]
Minority World	Often called 'developed countries, first world or the global north'. Only a small proportion of the world's population live in such countries.
Non-governmental organisation (NGO)	Is generally used to refer to charities working in development. An INGO refers to an international charity usually covering more than one country.
Self-help groups	Involve groups of people living in poverty putting their small weekly savings into a communal fund. This fund gradually increases and then is used to make loans to group members, usually to help them set up or build up a business.

All quotes are from the NIV Version of the Bible, unless otherwise noted.

---

[4] 'If all the world were a global village'
https://www.youtube.com/watch?v=A3nllBT9ACg three-minute film clip gives an indication of how people live across the globe.

CHAPTER 1
IT DOESN'T WORK

There's a problem… and it's a big problem.

So many of our well-meant efforts don't produce the kind of change that is needed. What's needed must be deep, broad and lasting.

But often the change that we bring is shallow, narrow and short-lived.

Let me illustrate this with a real-life story.

PERU, FEBRUARY 2015

Juan[1] is two years old and has big brown eyes. He is gentle, smiley – and ill. His intestines don't work properly and the town doctor says there is no hope for him. I'm on a work trip and have encountered many difficult situations but hadn't expected to meet such a devastating story.

As we visit his small home his mother's eyes fill with tears. I ask myself why he is sick. I don't know for sure, but I do know that he lives in a town where you can glimpse hell and that might be why.

Juan's home town of Challapata sits below vast spoil heaps from a mineral mine, one of the largest in South America. A river flows grey-black through the centre of town – it's more effluent than water. You wouldn't dare drink it. The air too is dangerous. Many people here die young from lung disease. I hear an ambulance siren; it means another miner has died. On average one miner dies every week.

Given these risks the miners are afraid. They seek protection by making offerings to a statue before they enter the mine. The idol is of the devil.

SO WHAT WOULD YOU DO TO HELP?

The most common approach would be to start a project[2] or give money for others to do so. The project would try to sort out some of the

---

[1] All the stories in the book are based on real people and places. However, I have generally changed names, locations and some details to preserve privacy.
[2] Projects are valuable for disaster-relief situations and for short-term change but they tend to have limited longer-term impact.

obvious problems: to provide money for Juan to get an operation, to pay for cleaning up the river and maybe to lobby the company to sort out safety in its mine. For a while it may work well and make a difference but what happens:

... for other sick kids in Challapata that the project can't afford to help?

... to address issues that the church or charity staff didn't know about or have not been able to focus on (such as the poor levels of education, tensions in the community or depths of despair)?

... when the river gets polluted or more miners die after the project has finished?

So, sadly, the change that we help bring is often shallow, narrow and short-lived. And we can easily feel overwhelmed by the problems of just one town. Let alone one country. One continent. Our whole world.

HOPE

My dream for Juan is that he will be able to flourish; that his family will be enabled to find and afford a skilful doctor or that God will heal him directly. I long for Juan to grow up in a Challapata that has been completely transformed. Where the river runs clear as glass, where all people are valued, where the schools thrive, where God, and not the devil, is honoured and where the sound of ambulance sirens has long since faded away. I long to see Juan's home town looking more like heaven than hell.

The challenge to bring deep transformation is encountered all across the world. Don't just take my word for it. Romnal Colas, Tearfund's Church and Community Transformation Lead for Latin America and the Caribbean, shares some insights from Haiti:

> *I was responsible, when I worked for another international non-governmental organisation (INGO), for coordinating the response to the devastating Haiti earthquake of 2010. We distributed cash, built temporary houses, constructed churches and dug wells.*

Our organisation decided to build twelve wells and identified twelve sites. We contacted the local pastors and told them we would like to provide wells, the only thing they needed to provide was the space for construction. We spent $3,000 on each well but, after less than one year, nine of them had stopped working.

I remember a conversation with Samuel, a wrinkle-faced pastor with a wide straw hat. He explained: 'Our well has not been working for over a month. The well is very important to us, we really appreciate that you gave it to us.'

I said: 'I don't understand, why have you not repaired this? It's just a simple seal that needs replacing.'

He explained: 'We thought you would come and take care of it.' They'd not contacted our organisation, they were just waiting.

Because we had the money, we had inadvertently become the 'big boss' with the power. So the decisions came from us: the US headquarters and the Haiti INGO office. We'd identified 'needs' but they were not necessarily the communities' priorities. They would accept the projects but didn't own the vision and didn't own the work.

Often our project managers wound up having to convince people to get involved. Communities frequently saw money from outside as a free resource and became dependent on it. When the projects ended, everything stopped. There was no further action or reflection.

Since that time, I have learned a completely different approach for working with communities. Instead of coming with your project ideas and plans you need to spend time with them, start with their own understanding and help them reflect on their situation. Coming to work with a community is like approaching a holy place. You need to take off your shoes and humble yourself.

There is hope for people like Juan in Peru and the people in Haiti. And for the people on your heart. 'Hope', not as we often use the word to mean a kind of wish, but biblical hope that is 'the confident expectation of what God has promised'.[3]

I know there is good reason to believe that transformation is possible.

Because of who God is and the promises of God's word. And because I have spent the last twenty years seeing this transformation happen all around the world through ordinary local churches.

I believe we sometimes overcomplicate how to bring positive change, and therefore think that only governments, large denominational development departments or charities can do what is needed. I'm not convinced that this is the case.

As I reflect on the last two decades, I am drawn to the simplicity of just three core principles:

> **God's vision:** We need to understand, be inspired by and work towards the wonderful fullness of God's kingdom vision of restored relationships.
> **All God's people:** In order to move towards God's vision, we need to value and mobilise each and every person made in God's image, work together in unity with our Christian sisters and brothers and with other people with godly values and make the most of all locally available resources.
> **Our God:** We need to place our trust and focus, not on ourselves, but in the calling, love, power and grace of our Almighty God.

I see these principles outworked, for example, in Jesus' feeding of the 5,000 – a miracle so important that it is found in all four of the gospels:

1. God's vision: The disciples needed to catch Jesus' compassionate and wider vision. Jesus called them to respond to the crowd's need to be reconciled to God and one another and for physical food.
2. All God's people. The disciples needed to find what local resources were available (two fish and five loaves), to bring

---

[3] Biblical Hope is defined in this article from *The Ecumenical Review* 5. 1 (October 1952), pp. 75-81.

those to Jesus and work together to distribute the bread and fish to the crowd.
3. Our God. The miracle did not happen because of the disciples' widened vision, important though that was. It did not happen because they made the most of local resources and worked together, important though that was. The miracle happened because of the character and power of God Himself in Jesus.

This book is in three parts. Each part considers one of the three principles: God's vision, all God's people, our God. I believe that these principles are the vital foundation for long-lasting transformation. And I hope by sharing and illustrating them that you and other readers may be encouraged and inspired as you bring change.

Each chapter generally covers a real story, reflections on that story and insights from friends and colleagues from around the world. I've used stories and kept the book brief to clearly highlight the core points and avoid over-complicating the ideas. As the scientist Albert Einstein once said: 'Everything should be made as simple as possible, but no simpler.'

May God speak to you through this book. To inspire you to help bring deep change that lasts with and for the people who are on your heart, whether they are local or far away. And so to contribute towards every person on planet earth experiencing a fuller life, from the life in all its fullness that Jesus brings (John 10:10).

But, before we go further, we need to ask ourselves an important question: what is the type of change that is most needed?

EXPLORING FURTHER
- Spend some time in a quiet place asking God to share more of his calling for you. You might also like to pray that God speaks to you through the words of this book.
- If you live in the Minority World, I recommend reading and responding to *When Helping Hurts: How to Alleviate Poverty Without Hurting the Poor … and Yourself*[4] which is a challenging and life-bringing book by Steve Corbett and Brian Fikkert.

---

[4] https://www.eden.co.uk/when-helping-hurts/

GOD'S VISION

Chapter 2
Where is life?

Cambodia, September 2018
I remember when our dream was ripped up, says Sopath.

We'd sacrificed so much to build our home. We'd been married for ten years when my husband Montha left Cambodia for better-paid work in Israel. I missed him so much I cried every day.

As I see Sopath leaning tenderly against Montha's arm, I can imagine how hard it must have been. We are eating rice and fish on a long table, sharing it with other members of their community.

Life was hard for Montha too. *I spent four years vaccinating chickens. I was not well treated, not the same as the Israelis. In our culture when people walk past we do not ask them, 'How are you?' We ask, 'Have you eaten?' and we invite them in to share our meal. But I wasn't allowed to eat with Israelis or even use the same knives and forks.*

I lived in Ramallah city. There was always conflict. I remember praying with other Christians as bullets skimmed overhead. I felt it was my one opportunity but it was very hard to live for so long so far away from home.

With the money Montha sent home, Sopath was able to finish building and decorating their house. It had a beautiful wooden floor and plenty of space for their four boys to play.

But Sopath also remembers the day that the tornado came. *I was at my father's house. It had rained for six days and then this incredibly strong wind hit our village. It tore down walls, pulled up trees by their roots and peeled the roof clean off our home like a lid from a can.*

This experience changed Sopath. *Is life in riches?* she ponders.

Chea joins our conversation. He's in his mid-twenties with an angular face and a wave of black hair swept across his forehead. *Young people round here don't know the purpose of life. They are addicted to mobile phone games. They don't know how to use anything but their thumbs!* As a father with two teenage boys I can relate to that!

We're all looking for life, whatever country we live in. We're thirsty people. But where is life?

The places we look for life are surprisingly similar, whichever part of the world we are from. We're drawn to security, significance and soulmates.

So we can look for life in the security of a house, possessions or job. Sometimes we look for life through our sense of significance – 'the status' of a job or a church or a community role. And we can look for life in our relationships with a spouse, partner, family and friends. These can all be good things – but are they life itself?

NUDGED OVERSEAS

Let me explain what I've discovered.

I used to work as a civil engineer. My job involved designing ways to protect people from flooding in South West England. I remember feeling quite satisfied when flood protection works were completed. Over several years I worked with a team to help protect the residents of the town of Perranporth from flooding, many of whom were elderly. I enjoyed my work, but I also asked myself, 'Do I want to work on this for the rest of my life?' And, 'How does my faith fit in?'

My thinking developed further during three weeks of voluntary work in the town of Dokolo in rural Uganda in 1995. I enjoyed the beauty, living simply and working alongside local students to help build college dormitories. Most of all, I relished time travelling with church members to meet, share with and pray with people in scattered rural communities.

I realised that I wanted to do work that wasn't just about bringing practical improvements to people's lives but also about helping them spiritually. So, four years later, I chose to leave my job for two years of voluntary work in Malawi.

WHAT IS DEVELOPMENT ALL ABOUT?

Malawi is known as 'the warm heart of Africa' because its people tend to be kind and welcoming. I settled into life in Zomba, a town on the lower slopes of a mountainous plateau.

My work was varied and rewarding as I helped design development projects and monitor their progress. Every project had a particular focus – such as building wells, helping people grow more crops or supporting people living with HIV/AIDS. Each had a solid plan and was led by staff with suitable expertise.

While the projects were active, I could see good results, but the initiatives always had limited lifespans. I also noticed there was a spiritual project helping rural clergy to more deeply understand the Bible. It was kept separate.

I really respected the people I was working with. However, I still wondered whether we were getting everything right. Did we understand the needs of the communities well enough? What would happen about things that were beyond the scope of the project? Would the benefits last after the projects finished?

And, more fundamentally, would we have truly served the people if all they experienced was more food and clean water? Life seemed to be about more than this. The most important part of my life was my relationship with God. Could we, or even should we, do anything about this relationship for or with them?

TRYING AND FAILING

This was how I wound up with my colleagues Thoko and Pemphero sitting on a grass mat in Mzembela community. We asked the people lots of questions about what they needed. The list they shared was mostly pretty familiar: clean water, more crops, better roads. They also shared about the challenge of monkeys coming to steal their crops. I don't think the conversation about spiritual needs got very far.

I pulled the various ideas together into a proposal called 'Kingdom Life'. My hope was that, through this project, this community would start to experience more of life in all its fullness.

But it didn't work out well. I'd failed to realise that we'd been directed to this community, not because of its depth of need but because it was the home village of a senior pastor we worked with. We'd just heard needs and nothing of what the community could do. I couldn't work out how to do anything positive to encourage faith. The project never happened and the community felt let down.

WRESTLING

I too felt disappointed and disillusioned with how we were doing development. I had a growing pile of questions about how we could truly serve communities. Foremost amongst them was why we, as a Christian charity, seemed to be focusing so little on spiritual needs. If a relationship with God is so vital, why was encouraging this not central to our work? What was going on?

EXPLORING FURTHER

- You might like to ask some people what they think life is all about. To what extent do their answers fit into security, significance and soulmates? How would you answer that question?
- Is it important for you to separate life into 'spiritual' and 'physical'? Take some time to look up the thirteen times that the word 'spiritual' occurs in the Bible and think about whether the Bible uses this word as a major division of life or just for specific situations.

CHAPTER 3
SHRUNKEN GOSPEL AND SLEEPING GIANT

ETHIOPIA, JULY 2018

I am chatting with Elder Tadele and Pastor Neberu, two church leaders in Bule Hora town in Ethiopia. Elder Tadele's face is round and he peers through glasses. Pastor Neberu is a younger man with high cheekbones. I sit on a plump, beige sofa.

We talk about looking after the environment. Elder Tadele shares that his church has planted some trees on the church compound. But he struggles to make a connection between this and his Christian faith.

Pastor Neberu, who is sitting next to me, joins our conversation. He makes a much stronger connection. *We are created to keep the environment well. Creation care is part of our calling as Christians. One part of the creation cannot live without other parts of creation. When we destroy the forest we cannot get the rain.*

Motivated by his beliefs, Pastor Neberu plans to make the expensive journey back to his home area, two hundred kilometres from Hawassa, to teach his people about the importance of caring for creation and therefore the need to stop destroying their local forest. He will also try to persuade the local government to take action to control the deforestation. I think that he is taking much greater action than Elder Tadele because he sees creation care as being core to his beliefs.

I wonder what your faith says about this issue? Is caring for the environment a central part of what it means to believe or an optional extra just for those who are motivated? I've changed what I believe. Let me tell you why.

FOOTPRINTS IN THE MILK

One bright April morning I opened our front door and saw strange footprints in a puddle of spilt milk. They weren't the right shape for our cat's paws or for the print of a dog or even a fox. I was excited to realise that they were the prints of a badger, an animal that is very rarely seen alive in the UK.

Why had this elusive creature visited us in the night? We had recently switched from buying supermarket milk in large plastic containers to getting milk delivered to our door in small glass bottles. And the badger had noticed, knocked over two bottles and enjoyed a drink.

My wife and I didn't make the change for the benefit of wildlife! We had previously thought a few times about getting our milk delivered. But, even though we knew glass bottles were recyclable and therefore better for the planet, we hadn't switched because of the increased cost. In this, as in many areas, my environmental commitment was sadly pretty shallow.

What had made me change my mind was hearing Dave Bookless, from A Rocha International, unpacking the Bible in a way I'd never heard before. As a Bible-believing Christian I had tended to understand the good news of the Christian gospel to be about a restored relationship with God. And it very much is. But the gospel also goes far further.

One of the best-known verses in the Bible is 'God so loved the world that he gave his one and only Son that whoever believes in Him shall not perish but have eternal life' (John 3:16). I'd always thought that the word 'world' here meant that God loved every single person on planet earth. Which He does and it's great. However, Dave Bookless explained that the original Greek word is 'cosmos' which means the whole of creation. Thus, Jesus died on the Cross so that the whole of creation, not just people, could come back into a vibrant relationship with God.

He then showed how important the environment is to God all through the Bible from Genesis to Revelation. And so he backed up, from the whole sweep of scripture, his assertion that the good news includes a restored relationship with our planet and all living things.

This had a big impact on me. No longer are environmental issues a peripheral part of my faith. Now they are central. I am more highly motivated to reduce my environmental impact, so we've switched to glass milk bottles, reduced our meat intake and reduced the amount we travel.

SHRUNKEN GOSPEL?

So why had I previously missed this aspect of the good news despite attending Bible-focused churches all my life? It all comes down to worldview. We all develop, over time, a way of seeing things that is influenced by our culture, education system, family, friends and coworkers. Some of this is so deeply ingrained that we are unaware of it. It's like if you wear a pair of dark glasses for a long time. You start to forget that what you are seeing is a filtered, reduced view of the world rather than reality.

Throughout my education and much of my church experience I had been taught to divide the world into the 'physical' (what you can see and test) and the 'spiritual' (what is invisible, deeper and connected with faith). I'd assumed that this way of seeing things came from the Bible. But I was wrong.

Five hundred years before the birth of Christ, the Greek philosopher Plato developed a way of thinking that separated the ordinary things we can see and interact with, such as a chair, and a perfect version of the same thing that exists elsewhere and invisibly.

This idea of separation was rediscovered during the European 'Renaissance', which lasted from the 14th to 17th century. The church took this thought and started teaching that the world was divided into the physical and spiritual. They took it further and said that the spiritual was more important than the physical. This is called 'dualism'. And dualism was taken by European missionaries across the whole globe.

WHAT DIFFERENCE DOES THIS MAKE?

A *huge* difference. Have you ever wondered why learning about faith in schools is usually kept just for religious education lessons? Religion is rarely if ever mentioned in lessons such as maths, science and geography. Why do many church denominations around the world separate their work into mission and development departments as if they were totally different things? And why do we have Christian 'relief and development' organisations split from 'mission' organisations?

In Ethiopia, our small group from Tearfund sat down with a group of very senior Christian development and denominational leaders to pray and to wrestle with theology and its practical implications.

Yonas, who heads the development department of one of the large church denominations in Ethiopia, told us: *Our denomination raises 90% of the funds needed for our evangelism work but has not, over fifteen years, contributed anything at all to the costs for development work. For this we totally rely on funding from abroad. For decades we have*

15

considered evangelism as spiritual work and therefore a core church responsibility. But serving people in poverty is 'development' and so, while it is a good thing, it is not really a vital part of the gospel and our faith. Some of us have been deeply concerned about this but this way of thinking is embedded in our church.

So Yonas was starting to realise that his denomination's dualistic view of the gospel resulted in little emphasis and practical action on restoring relationships with others, with themselves and with creation.

And this has lethal consequences. Salim, another senior church leader, came up to me during a coffee break and told me that two nominally evangelical Christian tribes in Western Ethiopia were currently fighting, resulting in hundreds of deaths and hundreds of thousands of people needing to flee.

And Ethiopia, like many Majority World countries, is scattered with the broken remains of well-meaning development projects, not locally owned and so rusting away.

When I started working for Tearfund I learned for the first time about 'integral mission'. The Lausanne Movement,[1] a global mission network, explains this:

> *Integral mission is defined as 'the task of bringing the whole of life under the lordship of Jesus Christ' and includes the affirmation that there is no biblical dichotomy between evangelistic and social responsibility in bringing Christ's peace to the poor and oppressed.*

> *This was further clarified at the 2001 meeting of the Micah Network in Oxford as 'the proclamation and demonstration of the gospel', emphasising that it is not simply the issue of evangelism and social involvement being done alongside each other but rather that 'our proclamation has social consequences as we call people to love and repentance in all areas of life' and that 'our social involvement has evangelistic consequences as we bear witness to the transforming grace of Jesus Christ'.*

This is life-transforming theology with great depths and richness. There is, however, a practical challenge. I have often found that the fullness of this theology starts to become lost at a local church and community level. So, for example, in Ethiopia I met local church staff who understood integral mission to mean that churches need to be

---

[1] https://lausanne.org/networks/issues/integral-mission

engaged in practical work to serve the poor. And it does – but it is broader than that.

Tearfund's understanding is that poverty is fundamentally the result of four broken relationships. The Bible describes how the Fall, in Genesis 3, led to broken relationships with God (8:23-24), with ourselves (8-10), with one another (16) and with creation (17-19).

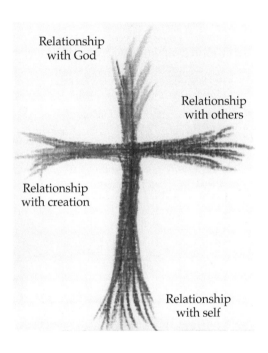

Yet through Jesus' death and resurrection God reconciled to himself all things (Col. 1:15-20). So now, through Christ, we can have a restored relationship with God (Col. 1:21-22), and from this we can have a restored relationship with ourselves (2 Cor. 5:17; 1 John 3:1), with one another (Eph. 2:19-22) and with creation (Col. 1:19-20). What wonderful, all-encompassing good news!

This wider understanding of the good news helps motivate Christians to get involved in all areas of life.

INSIGHT FROM ANNE MUMBI, TEARFUND ZAMBIA COUNTRY DIRECTOR

We need to catalyse the mind of the church itself. The church is in different places in Zambia. There's a segment of the church that believes that we cannot move without somebody giving us something.

But we, as Christians, need to walk out the four restored relationships that are in the gospel. We are a people in covenant with God and God could not walk into a community and leave it the same as it was before.

Chibolya is a settlement in the capital Lusaka. It's one of the most notorious in Zambia for drugs, gangs and crimes. Even politicians would fear to go there. But the Women of the Pan African Christian Women Alliance felt called to go there, so they did.

They linked up with the pastors of five local churches in Chibolya and the pastors, in turn, linked them with local community structures, including gang leaders. They're tackling Covid, which can spread like wildfire through such settlements, with face masks, sanitisers and health messages.

Even the Zambia National Broadcasting Corporation picked up on what was happening and started local TV programmes to support the sensitisation. 'Honestly, who goes into Chibolya? Only God.'

Rei Crizaldo is from the Philippines and works as Tearfund's Theological Network Engagement Officer for East and South-East Asia. He adds these thoughts:

Following Jesus is a major challenge in many parts of Asia where the church is in a minority. You give up a lot to become a Christian. If you are going to lose a lot, what life will you get? It's helpful to let people think about how important it is to let God into everything.

Do people think like we think? Do they separate food and God? Maybe in their mindset, how couldn't God be behind their food? Very few

---

---

people in Asia are atheists. It's great to put the God question into the story but not to isolate the relationship with God from the other relationships.

Jesus exemplified life with His gentleness and connection with the Holy Spirit. There are so many gods in Asia, the question is 'which one?' Jesus is so different and radical and so difficult to follow.

SLEEPING GIANT

How can Ethiopia be transformed? I believe that the deepest and most far-reaching way would be for the church to re-embrace the fullness of the gospel. And then live that out in every area of life.

For example, the beliefs and therefore the actions of the 70 million Christians in Ethiopia (65% of the total population) will substantially determine whether the environment there is cared for or destroyed. This is vital not only for the environment but also for the poor, who are the most likely to suffer and die because of drought, flooding and landslides.

Let's scale this up even further. There are about 2.4 billion people who classify themselves as Christians on the earth (33% of the world's population). The church is sometimes called the sleeping giant, due to our huge potential and more limited action.

What we, as Christians, believe and how we act will determine what kind of future there is. If we, as one third of the world's population, look after the planet well then that would have a massive positive effect.

But good theology makes little difference unless it is applied through effective discipleship – so that's what we'll turn to next.

EXPLORING FURTHER

- Consider Ruth Valerio's blog 'The Gospel, the Whole Gospel and Nothing but the Gospel'.[2] To what extent does this understanding of the good news fit with or challenge your existing understanding?
- Read Ruth's insightful book *Just Living*[3] and consider how to respond to the vision it provides of choosing simpler and more just lives.

---

[2] https://ruthvalerio.net/bibletheology/the-gospel-the-whole-gospel-and-nothing-but-the-gospel/
[3] https://ruthvalerio.net/publications/just-living/

CHAPTER 4
IF WE ARE TRUE BELIEVERS, THEN WHY ARE WE KILLING EACH OTHER?

SOUTH SUDAN, APRIL 2015

Paul is one of those people that you just warm to. He is broad-shouldered and gentle with a light-up-your-face smile. Paul was living in safety with his family in Canada but chose to move back to the war-ripped country of South Sudan.

How could anyone want to hurt this delightful man? They say in South Sudan that danger can spring out of nothing, like storm clouds from behind a mountain. Earlier, Paul and I had been watching kids laughing as they climbed trees in the town of Ibba. And now we are standing in a brick church building. We are talking with church members and are listening to their stories of war and change.

A man walks into the building dressed in dusty military fatigues. Tottering somewhat, he approaches us. His face is a deep ebony, the colour skin you need to withstand South Sudan's fierce sun. His eyes are glazed and I smell strong drink.

At first he talks fairly peacefully, even though his sentences are as jumbled as a pile of dirty washing. But then he mimes holding a rifle. He points it straight at the middle of Paul's chest. Paul's face freezes.

It's time to go, he says. At first I don't get it and carry on talking. But then I look at Paul's eyes and see deep fear. We quickly say our goodbyes and leave; our meeting lies abandoned behind us.

Paul has three parallel scars on his forehead. They tell the world that he is from the Dinka tribe, one of the two most powerful ethnic groups in South Sudan. But we've just been in an area belonging to the other most powerful tribe, the Nuer. And for this, the drunk soldier threatened to murder my friend.

As Paul and I travel away from Ibba through the wild bushland, he says something I will always remember. It's a question, mostly to himself: *If we are true believers, why are we killing each other?*

Paul then tells me: *The problem here in South Sudan is that churches have focused too much on making believers and not enough on making disciples. But there's a huge difference between the two. Believers say they have faith in God but many do not deeply change who they are and what they do. And, unless there's change, tribe comes first. Above anything else. Even God. And so when our tribe is threatened we kill each other and cause all this misery.*

The scale of the carnage shocks me. 383,000 people have been violently killed or have died because of illness or starvation caused by the war in South Sudan. Nearly 4 million people have had to flee. And seven out of every ten women sheltering in camps have been raped since the beginning of the conflict.[1]

True disciples of Jesus, the Prince of Peace (Isa. 9:6), wouldn't fight and kill in this way. And in their hearts they wouldn't put tribe above God. But they do. If we put anything above God then we are creating an idol (Exod. 20:3). *Discipleship is critical but we're not good at it*, says Theo, a friend of mine who is a South Sudanese Bishop.

A WIDESPREAD PROBLEM

As I travel the world, I realise that weak discipleship is not just a problem in South Sudan. It's everywhere, as shown in the following quotes.

> *Making disciples is the best way to counter extremism and terrorism and the best way to "stay above the water" in an atmosphere of secularism, atheism and capitalism.[2]*
>
> *Approximately half the population in this city are evangelicals. Yet this is the most unequal city in the country and for many years had the highest murder rate in the world.[3]*
>
> *In reality we are just not making the impact that we should ... In the church, when Jesus gives us an instruction, we feel we only have to memorise it.[4]*

---

[1] https://en.wikipedia.org/wiki/South_Sudanese_Civil_War
[2] Archbishop Moon Hing addressing a Mission Consultation Roundtable in Singapore, quoted in Anglican Communion News Service, Asia, '"Urgent need for discipleship", conference told', 20 October 2017:
https://www.anglicannews.org/news/2017/10/urgent-need-for-discipleship-conference-told.aspx
[3] Tearfund Country Director for Central America.
[4] Cris Rogers, *Making Disciples*, Cris Rogers (Sussex: Essential Christian, 2018).

> *We realise that some of the people in church have dodgy theology. For example, that women are second class people. Culture is in the church. We have wrongly assumed that because people are in the church they are being discipled.*[5]

The quotes are, respectively, from Asia, Central America, Europe and Africa. Rev. Canon John Kafwanka, the former Director for Mission for the Anglican Church worldwide, encapsulates the challenge as: *We as Christians, across the world, have so often spoken about Jesus Christ but we have never lived Jesus' way.*

OUR CALL TO MAKE DISCIPLES
Yet Jesus called his church to 'go and *make disciples* of all nations, baptising them in the name of the Father, Son and Holy Spirit, and teaching them to obey everything I have commanded you' (Matt. 28:19-20, emphasis added). To make *disciples*, not just believers.

You may, like me as a kid, have enjoyed singing 'The Wise Man Built His House Upon the Rock', and making as loud a clap as you could when the foolish man's house collapsed. Jesus explains in this story that we need to establish our lives by putting *into practice* his words (Matt. 7:24-27).

And, in John 15:5, Jesus elaborates on this when he says, 'I am the vine; you are the branches. If a person remains in me and I in them, they will bear much fruit; apart from me you can do nothing.'

The message is clear. If we want to see life-changing transformation in our world we need to grow as disciples. But how do we best do that? Here are a few principles:

GOD DISCIPLES US
One of my favourite paintings shows Jesus walking with two disciples on the road to Emmaus. This reminds me that the most important person I travel with, who helps me to grow, is God. Jesus called his disciples 'that they might be with him and that he might send them out' (Mark 3:14).

---

[5] Tearfund Project Officer for Zimbabwe.

COMPANIONS DISCIPLE US

I wonder what has helped you grow most as a disciple? I immediately think of Mark, my youth leader, who taught me when I was just fourteen to facilitate Bible study groups. Then, in my twenties, I remember sitting in Rev. John's book-filled study as he gently asked me about my life and walk with God and shared insights from his own experience. It's important that we have people who believe in us and help us grow.

DEVELOPING HEART, HANDS AND HEAD

Sometimes churches think that growing disciples is just about increasing people's knowledge and understanding of the Bible. However, a number of experienced practitioners talk of the importance of developing all three aspects of 'heart', 'hands' and 'head'. They remind us of the vital need for a living and experiential relationship with God (heart), of putting our faith into action (hands) and of deepening our knowledge of God's word (head).

BISHOP ANTHONY POGGO

Here are some insights from Bishop Anthony Poggo, who for many years was the Bishop of the Diocese of Kajokeji in South Sudan. He now advises Justin Welby, the Anglican Archbishop of Canterbury, on issues concerning the worldwide Anglican Communion.

Non-Christian culture has crept into our church in South Sudan. We see this in revenge attacks. These are very common in some parts of the country.

For example, the Kuku people of my home area of Kajokeji have a proverb that says, 'to pay back for your dead relative, you have to pay back by more than one' and so the brutal violence escalates. But this is not what the Bible teaches.

Fundamentally what is lacking in the church in countries like South Sudan is growth in Christian commitment.

How do we address this? I find a discipleship diagram, developed by the Christian organisation Navigators, very helpful.

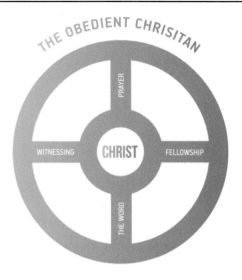

The hub of this wheel is Jesus. We need to be committed to Him. If there is no spiritual birth then there is no growth. In Him we are a new creation (2. Cor. 5:17).

Then discipleship needs to be intentional. The four important spokes that result in obedient Christians in action are:

Prayer

Ongoing daily prayer is the lifeblood of faith. To be filled with the Holy Spirit is a continuous process; we can't live on past events.

Word of God

The word of God is vitally important. As God says in Isaiah 55:11, 'My word that goes out from my mouth: it will not return to me empty, but will accomplish what I desire and achieve the purpose for which I sent it.'

In every culture we need to know how to handle the Word of God.

In communities where education levels are low it is very important to go slowly through the whole Bible and often use stories.

Community

Hebrews 10:25 says, 'Let us not give up meeting together, as some are in the habit of doing, but let us encourage one another – and all the more as you see the Day approaching.' The East African Revival, which started in the 1930s, was characterised by Christians meeting every week and being accountable to one another.

Whatever form it takes, Bible study groups, cell groups, WhatsApp groups, we need to meet regularly with other believers. And we need people to act as disciplers who have a concern for new Christians.

Evangelism

We are all called to witness and make disciples, as Jesus commands us in Matthew 28:18-20.

One way in which I saw transformation happening in practice was in the Church and Community Transformation work in my diocese and surrounding dioceses. The Word of God was transforming people.

When we do grow disciples successfully, what difference does it make? For example, can disciple-filled churches bring lasting hope in war-stained South Sudan?

SOUTH SUDAN, MAY 2015

Tonj is remote. We reach it by driving to the end of a road, then the end of a track, and lastly through the bush, following just a wandering path. Tonj's history is a sad one. In 1996 fighting swept through this village, the pastor was killed and everything was burned to the ground. *There were no more tukuls (thatched huts), only trees.*

The people fled and stayed away until the year 2000 when they cautiously started to come back. But how do you rebuild when everything's been destroyed? Pastor Deng is a tall man with a muscled back and warm face. He says, *We were cultivating 'small, small', just enough to eat but not enough to sell to cover other essential costs like school fees, salt or soap.*

Pastor Deng was discipled through reading what the Bible says about Church and Community Transformation[6] and by deciding to put that teaching into practice. One of the big challenges for Tonj village was the quality of their school. When they showed me and said, *Here is the government school,* I said, *Where?* You have to look hard to see it – it's just some warped benches under mango trees. And even then the school teachers don't always show up.

The church decided it was time for change. They shared their church building for the school to use and identified and sent three volunteer teachers for training. They also worked out a system where seventeen committed villagers volunteered to grow additional food to support the teachers. Now eighty children are benefiting and *even this year more are coming.* This type of change is more likely to last as there is no outside money involved.

The Anglican denomination wants to spread Church and Community Transformation across the whole of South Sudan. So you can start to see how this troubled nation could be changed from the grassroots up.

The international community contributes something like $560 million a year for relief for South Sudan. This provides key life-saving support. But, given that it keeps being needed each year, this money doesn't seem to be fundamentally changing the country. Maybe instead we need to increasingly look to ordinary people working as committed disciples with our extraordinary God, to bring the change.

This brings us to the end of Part 1 of this book. We've explored some of the profound problems associated with standard project approaches to try to bring transformation. We've considered how we tend to look for life in security, significance and relationships – but that life is ultimately found in God Himself.

We've challenged a common misunderstanding that divides the world into the physical and the spiritual and exhorts churches to focus primarily on the 'spiritual'. We've also explored a wider lens on the gospel, which talks about how Christ brings restoration of four key relationships: with God, ourselves, others and creation. This provides us with a broader view of the vision that God has for the world.

---

[6] See the Terms Explained table. CCT is also described in more detail in Chapter 7.

And in this chapter we've considered the vital importance and challenges of discipleship and some perspectives that can help us to develop ourselves and others as followers of Christ.

So now hopefully we have a clearer idea of what God is wanting wherever we are: the restoration of the four core relationships (Chapter 3). God tends to outwork his purposes through his church. Part 2 of this book considers who God's people are and how we need to work together.

EXPLORING FURTHER

- How does your church work to develop disciples? Which of the three aspects – heart, head and hands – tends to be most emphasised and which could benefit from more attention? *Making Disciples: Elevating the Conversation Around Discipleship and Spiritual Formation* by Cris Rogers provides a very accessible and practical guide to this, in fewer than eighty pages.
- What and who has most helped you to grow as a disciple? And how are you seeking to help others grow deeper in their faith?

ALL GOD'S PEOPLE

FOOTBALL WITH BLINKERS

NICARAGUA, NOVEMBER 2018

Have you ever found yourself shouting at a football player on TV to pass the ball? There's a teammate to their right in a carpark-sized space with a clear shot at goal. Yet the striker charges into a nest of defenders, head down and relying on their own dexterity. It usually doesn't end well.

I wonder if we, as churches, often play life in a similar self-focused way. We can think too much about our own projects and mission activities but miss what our sisters and brothers from other churches are doing in the same community, city or nation.

Maybe Martinez, Kristel and Sheryl, three brave young people from Nicaragua, can show us a better way. But first let's understand what they are up against.

I listened to Mario, a twenty-five-year-old young man with a smiling bright-eyed face. What he said was shocking. *I came from a struggling family. My mum had to be both Mum and Dad for me. She worked very long hours as a nurse. At secondary school I got involved in gangs. In my district there was lots of killing and I was part of this. I was becoming someone I didn't want to be, an animal. I was very lost in drugs and alcohol. I killed a man.* Just a kid but with blood all over his hands.

Many people tried to help Mario. *My elder brother's big mission in life was to rescue me. I was in a drug rehabilitation centre but not for long … I was in many homes and a psychiatric centre … But I arrived home full of drugs and I hit my Mum in the face.*

Nicaragua is wracked with such violence. You need to be brave to stand for something different.

Martinez is twenty years old and has an engaging smile and light in his eyes. *Many things churches do are just sticking plasters. But following the Transforma Joven (Transforming Youth) workshops we decided to do more. We developed an initiative called 'playing for peace'.*

It was aimed at preventing kids from joining the maras (gangs). Every week for three months we'd play twenty minutes of football then have a short reflection time and something to eat and then play football again. It gave the young people an alternative.

My area is one of the two most dangerous in the city. People are used to seeing lots of guns, gangs and violence. It's not easy. Last year I was threatened. One day the maras came into my house. Sometimes I'm afraid. Kristel and Sheryl, two sisters with beautiful long black hair, join in the conversation. Kristel says, *The challenge after we complete the training is to develop an initiative in our communities. We don't need a lot of resources. We have resources in our churches. We just need to work as a team. My brother (in Christ) has this skill and I have another. I believe at the end of this training we'll be like dynamite!*

I just finished the training last month, says Sheryl. I really liked that it brought together people from different denominations. It empowered sixteen-year-olds like me to share ideas about what we can do to transform our communities and country. We need to be 'salt and light' (Matt. 4:13-16).

We are working on a process for recycling and we want to avoid using Styrofoam. [Styrofoam is the 'disposable' white plastic that takes over five hundred years to degrade[1] and is used everywhere in Honduras, and in the USA]. *We plan to share environmental awareness in our city. We want to reach one hundred and fifty teenagers in our church. It's small steps but so exciting.*

May we be inspired by the example of these young people to be courageous and face what's wrong, even when it seems overwhelming. As Edmund Burke said, *'The only thing necessary for the triumph of evil is for good [women and] men to do nothing.'*

And may we, like Kristel and Sheryl, learn to work together in unity. Jesus believes unity is so important that he strongly emphasised it in his last major prayer before he went to the Cross: 'I pray … that all of them may be one' (John 17:20-26). Psalm 133 expresses eloquently the potential impact of such unity: 'How good and pleasant it is when God's people live together in unity … For there the LORD bestows blessing, even life forevermore.'

I think this unity needs to operate at three levels: i) within our local churches, ii) between different denominations and iii) throughout denominations and church networks.

---

[1] https://www.sciencelearn.org.nz/resources/1543-measuring-biodegradability

LOCAL CHURCH

We need to involve all people in the church, for everyone has something to contribute. 'Each of you has their own gifts from God' (1 Cor. 7:7). This includes the youngest and the oldest, the least and the most educated, those who stumble with words and those who soar with them, those who have obvious disabilities and those of us whose disabilities are more hidden.

I remember a child with Down's Syndrome who lived out warmth and trust in inspiring ways. My mother, even in her eighties, sat alongside young people and brought them her peace and a listening ear. And I recall a young guy in South Sudan who might have been easily overlooked, but whose pastor trusted to start a thriving business that part-funded the church. I wonder what similar examples you can think of.

BETWEEN DENOMINATIONS

We may be familiar with the picture of the church as the body of Christ as described in Ephesians 4:16: 'From [Christ] the whole body, joined and held together by every supporting ligament, grows and builds itself up in love, as each part does its work.'

I wonder whether we tend to apply this picture mostly to our own churches, and yet it can apply well across many denominations. I had to move towns frequently as part of my work and, as a result, worshipped with many different denominations. This experience helped me to see how much all Christian denominations have in common as well as the unique contributions they can make to the whole church.

For example, some denominations help us learn to develop solid biblical foundations for life, while others help us to connect with the mystery and glory of God or the intimate relationship that He offers. Some encourage us to worship exuberantly and others to meditate, ponder and lament. Others are particularly inspiring at practical action or lobbying for justice. When all these parts of the body of Christ are brought together in unity then a wonderful potential is released.

Sometimes churches can feel nervous about working with other denominations due to doctrinal differences or concerns that the other church will take members of their congregation ('sheep stealing'). Often, I think the key barrier is that the leaders of local churches from different denominations or church networks don't know one another.

As local church leaders make the effort to get to know one another, trust can be built and it becomes more possible to identify areas where they can cooperate without compromise. We usually have more in common than we might think.

DENOMINATIONS AND CHURCH NETWORKS

When whole denominations or church networks become fully involved, then really large-scale change becomes possible. Such change tends to far exceed what can be brought about through individual organisations' projects.

Let's hear some other perspectives, this time from Brian Fikkert, President of the Chalmers Center in the USA and co-author of the book *When Helping Hurts*.

I am not very good at unity. By nature I am highly individualistic. I think that part of this is due to being much younger than my siblings, so I was raised as almost an only child.

As a result, I find Jesus' prayer for us in John 17, with its view of flourishing as a tangled, spaghetti bowl of relationships, to be somewhat strange. Does John 17 give us any insights into the reason that the movement restrictions during Covid have been so difficult? Everyone's fatigued, weary, frustrated. Why?

There are three different stories[2] going around about who we are.

The first story, which is at the heart of my discipline of economics, says that human beings are fundamentally autonomous, self-interested, material creatures, so happiness comes from greater individual consumption.

If this story, Western Naturalism, is true, then Covid lockdown shouldn't bother most of us, because we've been able to go on consuming just as we did before. In this story, the relationships

---

[2] For more on these three stories, see Brian Fikkert and Kelly M. Kapic, *Becoming Whole: Why the Opposite of Poverty isn't the American Dream* (Chicago: Moody Publishers, 2019).

envisioned in John 17 would not entail flourishing; they would be a living hell.

The second story tells us that we are autonomous, self-interested, material creatures that also contain souls that can have a relationship with God. This framework, Evangelical Gnosticism, is basically just Western Naturalism with a soul tacked on.

It results in Sunday church-going and worship, but on Monday to Saturday we revert to chasing 'The American Dream' of life, liberty and the pursuit of individual happiness. Sadly, this story is rampant in the Western church, and I find that it is deep within me. Again, this story can't explain the pain of Covid, because Covid hasn't prevented most of us from praying once a week and pursuing individual material prosperity the rest of the week.

The third story is the only true one. We are deeply created for relationships, as we see in the beautiful image of God dwelling with people in deep community in the Garden of Eden and in the new creation described in Revelation 21.

This way of seeing life means that John 17 makes total sense. It's God's vision. We are not created for individualism, we are created for community. And this is why the separation of the Covid restrictions are so painful.

And so unity is the vision that Christ has for us. We have to pursue unity if we are going to be in tune with God's mission. When we try to build bridges with others, we are doing God's work.

I have to work at being the welcoming committee. There are two keys for unlocking unity. The first key is that unity is a family commitment, not an optional extra. As the body of Christ, we are part of the same family. It's not a choice; it's a reality.

The other key is, as Westerners, to repent of our materialism and of seeing ourselves in a position of superiority. No-one's superior in the body of Christ, we are all made in the image of God and called to embrace one another as sisters and brothers.

Churches can still feel overwhelmed by the scale of needs around them. Fortunately, God has a bigger team than we often realise. God's people also include people with kingdom values who don't yet know the King.

EXPLORING FURTHER

- Find out about what other local churches in your area are working on and aiming to do. Are there areas of common agenda with your church?
- How might you be able to learn from one another and encourage these other local churches, as together you seek to serve God?

CHAPTER 6

WE CAN'T CHANGE THE WORLD

WEST AFRICA, MAY 2013
I watch as Pastor James, a short man in a bright purple shirt, brown trousers and glasses, drinks water from a newly built well. Women, in the crowd that surrounds us, dance exuberantly and sing *We have water, we are happy.* You need to know some background to realise the fullness of what is happening here.

Gola was a neglected community. Pastor Timothy says: *We were in darkness. No government people have come here since the civil war* [which ended in 2002]. And it was a divided community.

Relationships around the world between Christians and Muslims are quite often strained. The Sahel, the wide band of land just south of the Sahara Desert in Africa, is one place with particular inter-faith challenges. These strains are often part of a complex political, tribal and livelihood dynamic.

In Gola, Adama, the pastor's wife, explained that previously, *if any of the Muslim children came to church their parents would beat them.* In turn, the church *was just inward looking.* And yet the two faith communities shared some common challenges.

Water was a major problem. Lilian says, *I used to walk two miles to get water from an open well or streams and carry it back on my head. It took two hours to get it, including time to queue, so I was losing important time for farming. My children used to get sick a lot and we had periodic outbreaks of cholera.*

When the church started to reflect, as part of a Church and Community Transformation (CCT) initiative (see Chapter 7), they grasped the idea that, *the water we drink is life.* And that, *when sickness comes it comes not just for Christians or for Muslims but for all. So we need to work together to address our problems.*

Chief Abdul rises to speak; his long green robe conveys something of his natural dignity. *Since time immemorial we have had a problem with getting pure water. Last year there was an outbreak of cholera in this area. At first, when the church approached us to work together, I was sceptical. I wasn't sure that we would find water but now the well is finished.*

We are grateful to God through the church for providing us with this water. Water is life. We decided that Pastor James should be the first person to taste the water as the church was the source of this blessing.

MORE IN COMMON

By working with the whole community, across divides of faith, gender, age or ethnicity, more people and resources become available to contribute to initiatives.

When people get to know and work with others who are different, misunderstandings can break down. As a colleague of mine says, *You overcome prejudice one relationship at a time.*

Often we realise that we have more in common than we might have thought. In Gola, for example, both faith groups were involved with rites of passage for young girls that included female genital mutilation (FGM). Adama explained that *These activities involved big dances and lots and lots of rice and so were very expensive. Now, instead of using our resources to hurt our children, we can use the money for their education. Previously we thought that girls were not meant for education but now there are more girls than boys at the school.*

OVERLOOKED PEOPLE

In Angola different divides needed to be overcome. We were met by a large crowd in a dusty village. It was much too large a gathering to properly hear people's experiences. So we asked the group to divide up into youths, women and men.

We soon realised that, while some of the men were good at making speeches, few of them had actually been involved in bringing change. The women were clearly passionate, had strong ideas and were much more engaged. They had helped identify the problem of inadequate numbers of classrooms at the local school and had mobilised everyone to build additional classrooms with some support from the local government.

However, the young people we met were angry. *The community used us when they needed people to do the heavy work of carrying sand or water but never involved us in decision-making.*

It is all too easy to overlook less vocal parts of societies, especially when power is reinforced by local culture. I wonder who are the overlooked people where you live and what valuable insights they could bring?

SERVING FIRST

Sometimes the church has too poor a reputation to be accepted as a co-worker with the wider community. In such instances it may be best for the church to start by serving that community. This shows the church's positive intentions and establishes initial relationships.

One such instance was in a community I visited in Nepal.

The Hindu members of the community originally thought that *Christians are a disease*. It is hard to believe that this small group of believers in Nepal had such a bad reputation. Pastor Kancha Bahadur and his wife Batuli have just welcomed us into their home and served us a generous lunch of goat curry, water chestnuts and rice. I guess the wider community didn't yet know their generosity and love.

When, in 2015, a major earthquake struck, the congregation responded by sheltering fifty people in the church, giving blankets for warmth and sheeting to start rebuilding their homes. The wider community saw that these Christians cared about them and so relationships started to improve.

Nowadays that church is a channel of all sorts of blessings. Inspired and trained through Church and Community Transformation (see Chapter 7), they work with their neighbours to help start goat rearing, beekeeping and vegetable growing as ways to improve their lives. Shyam demonstrates making bricks using hand-worked machines for sale at 60 rupees (45p) per brick.

The church has also worked to repair and upgrade the local road so that the vehicle that collects milk can access the area even in the monsoon. When asked what keeps him persevering, Pastor Kancha Bahadur says, *I want to be like Jesus, caring for the poor and being part of their struggles.*

SHARED KINGDOM VALUES

It is usually possible and helpful to work with other people who share kingdom values even if they do not yet know the King. This means we may well find we have common interests in addressing relationship issues to do with self, others and the environment (i.e. three of the four core relationships we considered in Chapter 3).

We could, for instance, work with a secular organisation that works to improve mental health (and so helps restore a relationship with the self). Or cooperate with a mixed network of organisations that are working to end conflict (so helping restore relationships with others).

However, it is important for churches to also clearly maintain their own Christian identity and their focus on the restored relationship with God. There is a risk that plans developed with those of no faith or other faiths might lead towards a vision of the future that is only concerned with material changes or that restricts opportunities to sensitively share one's faith with others.

While working together with others it is vital that local churches maintain their commitment to foundational practices of discipleship, including understanding and applying the Bible, worship and prayer.

Insights from Levourne Passiri from Chad, West Africa:

Before Church and Community Transformation (CCT), people used to drink water from rivers or ponds, together with their animals … They suffered a lot from diarrhoea, stomach aches and vomiting.

The church was distant from the wider community and wondering how to bridge the divide. Two initiatives that proved to be very helpful were the CCT approach and the local house of prayer[1] (LHop) approach, working in an integrated way.

People didn't have the resources for transformation but when the two concepts (CCT and LHop) were introduced it became easier to raise the funds … People here testify to the way the Lord is blessing them and so enabling them to give.

That was when they started to see results with the village chief, who was from a traditional belief background. The facilitators' ideas were then accepted easily. The village chief asked forgiveness for not considering the church and all that it could bring. The chief has now become a Christian.

Together they found a teacher who was not a Christian to lead the school in the church building. Now he is a Christian! The school has

---

[1] https://www.localhousesofprayer.org/

---

been integrated into the government school system. The community is now raising funds for training one of their community to be a nurse.

Makeure shows some of the deepest community transformation in Chad. People have come to faith, relationships within the community have moved from distant to close, girls are now receiving education, more than fifty trees have been planted, a primary and secondary school, a borehole and sand-dam have been built and people's confidence has grown both in God and themselves. There are also several inclusive and mixed community groups running self-initiated projects.

We can attribute a lot of this change to the local house of prayer approach. There is a difference between just CCT and CCT with LHops. The LHop in Makeure is key to not only personal transformation, but also transformation of the community.

We can see that the team to bring change can be much broader than we might have imagined. Now we need to consider what each of us brings that will help improve lives.

EXPLORING FURTHER

- Which other groups or individuals in your area have some kingdom values?
- How might you explore working with them on issues where you have common aims? What risks might you need to be careful of?

CHAPTER 7

FIVE LOAVES AND TWO FISH

Patricia felt cool wet mud on her cheek. She was lying on the road. At night. Mud was caked in her hair and smeared into her dress. Her head was spinning and her thoughts seemed as dark as the surrounding fields. Somewhere up ahead her husband Peter was leaning against a tree being sick.

Again. She was here again. Patricia knew this pattern.

They had nothing, just the worst land in the village, covered in boulders and a mud hut that let in ropes of rain.

Every so often Patricia and Peter would somehow gather together a small amount of money. Perhaps from selling the last of their furniture or cooking pots. Then they'd sit around a shallow communal bowl of local spirits, slurping it up through a long plastic straw and passing it on to fellow drinkers.

The drink would burn hot in her mouth and then fill her body with warmth. For a while her worries would sink back into the corners of her mind. But such evenings always ended up here, blind drunk.

Yet, even as she slumped in the mud, she remembered her sister's words: *You don't have to be a drunk, Patricia, it's not who you really are. I've been going to these village meetings and they say we can be like lights in our community. I don't fully get it, but it sounds good. Why not come along?*

The next week Patricia did try the meetings. Over the subsequent months she started to learn that she had more than she thought. And that she could change her situation and bring change with God and the support and encouragement of the church and community.

At one of the meetings Patricia had been saying, *It's all very well saying we all have resources when you've got good land, but ours is blistered with boulders. How can we grow anything on rock?!*

Violet, an older lady with bright eyes and a withered left arm, spoke up: *But those rocks are useful! You can break them up into small stones and sell them to those people who are building the road. God's given you your five loaves and two fish!* Villagers Gregory and David chipped in saying, *And we'll help you break the rocks up, we've got two solid hammers ...*

So Patricia, and eventually Peter, with their new church and community friends, did break up those boulders and got some money. This time they didn't spend it on drink. With their new hope, support and prayer they both were beginning to leave alcoholism behind them – investing the money from the rocks into buying and breeding chickens.

Once they'd sold plenty of chickens, they were able to buy three pigs and some goats. When I met Patricia and Peter, they had fattened the pigs up and were preparing to take them to market.

I was struck by how well the couple looked, both of them beaming with smiles. Patricia in particular looked resplendent in a beautiful white dress with a purple flower design. We sat in the shade of a mango tree and chatted.

Peter explained that over the years both he and his wife had come to faith in God and were now flourishing. He loved the idea that he could help the community be a good place, like salt helps meat to stay wholesome. In fact, it was this verse from Matthew 5:13 that had triggered him to come back to faith. And he had determined that his wife would change from being dressed in dirty rags to being *the best-dressed woman in the village*. And she was!

I love seeing this kind of change in people's lives.

The meetings they had attended were part of the Tearfund-supported process Church and Community Transformation (CCT). This can be simply understood as three stages:[1]

---

1) CATCHING A VISION

Facilitators help local churches to catch a broader and empowering vision of what God's kingdom would look like in their locality. God does this through the whole congregation participating in understanding and applying selected Bible passages.

---

[1] Tearfund understands CCT to be bounded by six principles. Appendix 1 shows how the three main principles in this book relate to Tearfund's six principles.

This is why the church in Patricia and Peter's village had been considering Jesus' teaching about being like salt and light in communities. Other life-transforming passages that are used include the Good Samaritan, Jesus feeding 5,000 people and Elisha, the widow and her oil.

The word of God has tremendous power to bring change, particularly when people engage with it directly. In many places the word is just preached from the front of church. This is valuable but it is even better when members of the congregation are enabled to study the Bible

directly for themselves. The messages from God's word go deeper into their hearts.

---

2) BUILDING COMMUNITY, UNDERSTANDING AND PLANS

This involves:

- building relationships with the wider community
- understanding the challenges and opportunities of the local context (through simple participatory rural appraisal approaches)
- jointly developing a vision and plans for change.

As the local church took biblical messages to heart they started to look out more compassionately to the wider community. They started to welcome and care for people on the margins, such as Peter and Patricia.

Peter and Patricia in turn experienced a profound shift in their whole way of seeing life. They'd moved from despair, thinking that they couldn't change their situation and had nothing, to hope and realising they did have resources and could change things.

The process told us we cannot wait for someone to come, we are to be salt and light in the world ... and it has helped us to understand that we have many resources to help ourselves.

This is a vital shift in perspective. Sadly, so many people living in poverty in both the Majority and Minority parts of the world don't think they can change their situation. Instead, they tend to look only to a rich relative, a government or a charity to bring change. And yet we are all made in the image of God and can bring transformation.

---

3) USE LOCALLY AVAILABLE RESOURCES TO TURN THE VISION INTO REALITY

- These include human, social, economic, physical, faith and time.
- They can also include the resources available from local government and other charities.

This new way of thinking about resources had enabled Patricia and Peter to realise the value of their boulders, to make the most of the money from the sale of the resulting construction gravel and then steward the chickens, goats and pigs.

They'd also experienced the value of encouragement, ideas and prayers from their group. Their lives and the lives of their ten children had been transformed.

Now they have plenty of plans for the future. They want to make the most of a small shop they have set up to sell clothes, cosmetics, salt, soap and paraffin.

When we parted company, Peter's face beamed with joy and he blessed us with a generous gift of a chicken and some eggs.

Here are some further insights from Dr Florence Muindi, founder and CEO of Life in Abundance, based in Kenya.

When I started out, I thought that I was well equipped to serve because of my training as a medical doctor and my Masters in Public Health. However, in Ethiopia I learned that change cannot just be about what I can share, or even just about a mobilised community.

Work that is not connected to local church, church leadership and spiritual formation tends to become an end in itself and will, with time, fade away. It's like a branch not connected to the vine.

I've learned that we need to equip the institution that the Lord said he would establish his work on. The local church is the number one local resource and needs to be the centre and the foundation for everything we do.

We start with prayer walking, seeking to discern what is God's agenda for a given community and what He is inviting us to join in with. We then seek relationships with a range of local churches and host a visioning forum.

In due course we help churches and communities to identify a range of resources, including people's talents; systems of government, education and empowerment; natural resources and physical assets, and networks such as complementary NGOs and organisations to whom we can refer communities.

We often see local resources multiplying over time. For example, we worked in a semi-arid part of Kenya where the felt need was for better food security. The community had a problem: when they tried to store grain it became infested with weevils. As a result they had to sell their crop soon after harvest to a middle man and then buy back grain, later in the year, at a high price.

Through the initiative, the church formed a church-based association that constructed an effective grain store, committing to sell back grain during the dry season at a price set in advance by the community. The church thus became a local custodian of justice.

In time, the profits from selling grain meant that a second round of silos could be constructed and then, later on, they had enough finances to buy a tractor and to construct boreholes. So what had started as a problem was addressed using local resources which, in turn, grew over time.

BROAD, DEEP AND LASTING CHANGE

In Chapter 1, I argued that we need to see the broad, deep and lasting change that is needed. Do CCT approaches result in such change?

Research on CCT carried out by independent consultancies is very positive:

Depth of transformation: 'The results provide clear evidence that the CCT process is having a positive impact on individuals and communities … The outcomes mentioned most often were an increased feeling of empowerment, self-worth and confidence, and improved community relationships.' Uganda QUIP Study Report

Breadth of transformation: 'The research identifies a wide range of poverty indicators for which improvements were linked to participation in CCT, and these indicators cover all aspects of the holistic understanding of poverty proposed for the research (material, wellbeing and spiritual).' GAMOS, An evidence-based study of the impact of church and community mobilisation in Tanzania, Executive Summary

Length of transformation: In 'Longer Term Sustainability of the CCT Programme' GAMOS concludes: 'there is little evidence that positive change achieved by the programme has fallen off after completion of the programme.'
The impact data for 61% of the communities was from between three and six years after 'programme' end.

When communities genuinely and deeply own initiatives, then sustainable transformation becomes much more possible, even in the face of huge challenges.

Uwero, a community in North East Uganda, illustrates this. Initially the people there felt very dependent on outside support. For instance, one-time Tearfund's local partner, Pentecostal Assemblies of God (PAG), had given selected community members cassava seedlings to grow to diversify their crops. A couple of months later weeds started to come up in their cassava fields and they contacted PAG and said, *Come and weed your crops!*

However, things started to deeply change when this same community took part in CCT. The adults decided, *we do not want our children to be as poor as we are and so we are going to build a good school here*. At the time their children were walking a three-hour round trip to the nearest school and were arriving too hungry from the journey to study well.

So this group decided to build a school in their village and made a large mudbrick and thatched structure. But just three months later Karamojong cattle raiders swept into the village and burned the school buildings to the ground.

Everyone fled for their lives. When things settled down they cautiously returned. And once again they said to themselves, *we do not want our children to be as poor as we are and so we are going to build a good school here.* Then they got back to the hard work of rebuilding the school.

Sadly, over the next few years this community underwent attacks from the vicious militia group the Lord's Resistance Army, the Karamojong raiders once more, and government troops running amok.

Each time the school was destroyed or badly damaged, but each time the people rebuilt it, with their own words resonating in their heads: *we do not want our children to be as poor as we are and so we are going to build a good school here.* The change in the community was mostly in people's thinking and motivation. So when they fled they took this thinking with them and when they returned they brought back their passion for improvement. Now that's what I call lasting change!

Sometimes, however, problems are so big that we need help from businesses and governments – so how do we work successfully with them?

EXPLORING FURTHER

- Tearfund Learn provides free access to a wealth of resources on how to mobilise churches to bring transformation at Tearfund Learn - Church and Community. These resources include toolkits for inspiring church leaders, the church and community mobilisation process (CCMP) that is used widely across Africa, and Umoja, a Church and Community Transformation approach used in Asia and Latin America.[2]
- You may like to also consider some similar approaches, including Reconciled World's Truth-Centered Transformation, Mothers' Union's Metamorphosis, Samaritan's Purse's Raising Families and the Salvation Army's Faith-Based Facilitation.

---

[2] https://learn.tearfund.org/en/

CHAPTER 8
MY MONEY IS IN THE WORLD

RECIFE, BRAZIL 2015

Floodwater stinks. Floodwater ruins. Floodwater can kill.

Imagine that you live in Coqueiral, a poor suburb of Recife in Brazil. You work three jobs to earn enough to live and feed your kids. You're permanently tired. Slowly, ever so slowly, you've managed to save enough to buy a few chairs and a battered fridge.

One night you wake up and sense something is wrong. Smell something is wrong. The River Tejipió always stinks but it's five hundred metres away, so the smell is usually bearable. But not tonight. Tonight the River Tejipió is downstairs, flowing through your home.

In the morning you and Juan, your brother, consider the damage from last night's flood. Luckily all your family survived but your dog Pepé was washed away and drowned. The two chairs that were downstairs are drenched in muddy water. You clean out your fridge and try plugging it back in. There is a spark, a bang and a small plume of acrid smoke. Wrecked.

What will you do now? You can't afford to move anywhere else. You live in this part of the city because it's cheap. But it's also dangerous. Here gang leaders drive slowly in their four-wheel drive trucks, guns held casually out of the window.

Here there are far too many red lights after dark. Here you can look down a side-street and spot clumps of kids blank-eyed on drugs.

And what about your kids: Claudia, Patricia and Ernesto? What hope is there for them when there are too few jobs and too many temptations?

A week later and you're sitting towards the back of a meeting of the local Baptist church. The building is quite impressive with its high roof and egg-shell blue walls. The conversation is, however, becoming heated.

But what are you going to do about the floods, pastor? asks Paula, who's a mother with her youngest child wriggling near her feet.

Well … I'm not sure that's my role. I'm here to preach the good news. The pastor is a good man and clearly deeply challenged.

What good news is it if we all drown! calls out Paula.

You know what I think? says Rodrigo, an elderly man with a cascade of white hair. He speaks quietly and slowly, picking his words. But, because it's him, most people listen.

I've worshipped in this church for nearly eighty years. I've heard God's word all that time. We're meant to be good neighbours, we're meant to serve like our Lord and wash feet. But I think we're not living all those words.

We know the problems, it's not just the floods. But what difference do we make as a church? If we disappeared one day, would the community around us notice? Would they?

He looks around at all who have gathered. Everyone's silent but everyone knows the answer. It's 'no'.

So Baptist Coqueiral Church started on a long journey. I caught up with them in February 2015. The main building doesn't look like a church to me. It looks like a large, open-sided shed. There are a few scattered chairs inside and a small group of young people shooting basketballs at a hoop to one side.

Pastor José, a man with an animated face, picks up the story: *From 2002 to 2006 we reflected and prayed a lot. By 2006 we decided that if we wanted to stop the cycle of poverty we needed to invest in the children for the long term.*

But how? We didn't have money, most of our one hundred and fifty members were poor. So we prayed. Eventually we sensed God saying to us, 'My money is in the pocket of the world.'

We started to help the young people to learn well and become citizens of good character. We now serve six hundred young people.

We realised that our church building was getting in the way of us being God's house. So we knocked down the building. Now we have a church space where we can worship and the young people can play football and basketball.

And we can provide shelter for families when there is a flood. When the river floods, we stop what we are doing and give up the church area so people can come here to stay, sleep and cook until the water goes down.

By 2008 the kids were starting to do much better but the parents were still struggling. So we started an initiative called 'working together'. Through this, young people, from fifteen to thirty years old, are trained and this helps them to find jobs. 30% of them gain jobs even during the course, we don't know how many afterwards. Coca Cola supports this initiative.

Our other supporters for income generation and apprenticeships are Caixa Econômica (Brazil's fourth biggest bank) and Gerdau, Brazil's largest steel company. So you can see how God's 'money is in the pocket of the world'!

Before we got involved, 20% of the local kids were using drugs. Now in our programme only two are using drugs and we're trying to help them get free. Around here 7% of young girls would on average become pregnant while still in school but it's down to 1% for those we work with.

In 2010 we started facing another challenge. We were doing fine, we were taking care of the poor but not treating the causes. We understood there is a machine that creates poverty. We need to help people see the challenges of the structure and act against this to stop poverty.

We needed to address poverty thoroughly, so we launched the 'school of faith and citizenship' to develop our understanding.

Critical factors that have led to this wide-reaching and effective work from a modest poor church are:

1) **Prayer.** In 2002 they did a lot of all-night prayer vigils. Nowadays they pray two hours every Monday and Friday and at least four times a year have all-night prayer vigils (10pm to 5am). Prayer involves them with God and brings them together as people.

2) **Sharing the vision repeatedly** with the church's small group (Bible study group) leaders.

3) **Living and working in unity with other churches.** Before this, local churches did not work together. Sadly, there were personal kingdoms that were bigger than God's united kingdom.

There is now very good communion between churches. They come from a wide range of church traditions – some are Pentecostal, some traditional, it doesn't matter. *Naturally we help each other, even personally, pastor to pastor we take care of each other.*

Now, every year, we do a joint church march against violence. We shut the churches on Sunday evenings and march together then worship together. 2,000 people take part, it's the biggest annual social movement.

The kingdom is made with many hands.

4) **Crisis.** *If the church does not face a crisis, it will not change. I love crisis. If there isn't one the pastor needs to bring one! Crisis is the embryo of change if you are up for the fight. Every crisis is a new step, it's a constructive crisis. I am writing a new book called 'Sorry To Disrupt You, We Are Changing'.*

5) **Deeply changing thinking.** They believe that *'every practical change without the ideas of change will fail'*. They share the ideas first and the activities are birthed in this.

The most precious thing about this church is not the actions, even though they help 1,400 people directly. The most precious thing is the understanding of the church that this is not just the social work of the church, but it is a way of being church.

Levels of violence in the area are now much lower. This has had some interesting results. More shops have moved into the area and house prices have increased. The price of a house about one kilometre away from the church would be $R 70,000 (about £15,000) but the same house near the church would now be $R 250,000!

This year the practical focus as churches together is flooding. *We have a really big problem here as every year people build closer and closer to the river. But every year in the winter this area floods and about 10,000 people are affected; last year three people died in the floods. We will get together to work on this. The problem is that the City Hall does not collect the trash here and the community put the trash in the river, which blocks it up.*

We are working on a campaign: 'Clean River, Healthy City'. We will educate the community on recycling and where to put the trash and we will work to push the local government to do what it should do. The churches are going to schools to reach the kids and teachers.

So we can see that, when an ordinary church led by God works with businesses, local government, other churches and the community, then many things become possible.

We do, however, need to be aware of some of the potential problems of working closely with businesses and government. Businesses are likely to have a commercial agenda and so churches need to be careful of where boundaries are needed to protect possibly vulnerable people from inappropriate marketing.

With governments, churches need to be aware of the degree to which government officials are genuinely interested in supporting community improvements and how much of a personal political agenda is present. It is generally wise to avoid association with particular political parties.

This type of transformation is good news for people in the Majority World but what about communities in the Minority World?

Can applying similar principles change such countries or are the situations too different?

EXPLORING FURTHER

- Which local or national businesses could you partner with as you work to bring transformation? What risks might you need to be careful of?
- Tearfund's 'Bridging the Gap Report'[1] explores the role of local churches in fostering local-level social accountability and governance.

---

[1] https://learn.tearfund.org/en/resources/policy-reports/bridging-the-gap

CHAPTER 9
THE SAME CALLING

Batman and Robin are wading through muddy floodwater. It's the middle of the night and pitch black. They are trying to pull up a drain cover. They are working to release floodwater and protect nearby homes. The difference between Batman and Robin's usual adventures[1] and this one, is that this one is real.

The story begins with a gate. When David (locally nicknamed 'Batman') started as the local Church of Ireland minister he discovered that the main gate to the church was always shut and locked at night. This was to keep out the local youths and was an understandable precaution. The area had a bad reputation – it was in the worst 10% for anti-social behaviour in East Belfast. The local kids would hurl stones at the police. But keeping young people out doesn't fit with Jesus' open-handed example.

David decided to keep the gate open. Many of the young people wound up joining a vibrant church youth club. The area now has some of the best social behaviour in East Belfast and some of the lowest numbers of burglaries in the whole of the UK.

How did that happen? Three things stand out:

Simple service: The church's attitude became *'what can we do to help?'* This meant, for instance, assisting with sports activities at the local school, handing out bags of salt during a bad winter and lobbying for a new football pitch to replace the existing one that was covered in shattered glass.

Faith: John ('Robin'), the church's community worker, says, *Pray for a vision from God and stick to that vision* and *prayer has to be the centre of whatever you do*. A local house of prayer approach was key.

Working with others: The church worked with a nearby supermarket to help people with food and cleaning materials after the flood, met the local water authority to sort out the underlying flooding problems and helped set up a joint community forum to address local issues.

---

[1] Batman and Robin are the names of American comic superheroes. Here they are the nicknames of the Church of Ireland minister and the church youth worker.

The attitudes and actions of this church in Northern Ireland remind me of the description of the early church in Acts Chapter 2: a Christian community characterised by deep faith, unity, generosity and concern for the poor. When local churches live this out, people from outside the church are attracted to what is happening and become more open to respond to God.

I notice that the approach that took this church in the Minority World out into its community looks pretty similar to the ones I've seen in the Majority World. I'm not surprised as people are people wherever they are, and the principles of God's word are equally applicable everywhere. They apply in my own village in the UK.

My village sits in a valley. To the north stretches the sharp edge of a line of hills called the North Downs. The community includes everything from five-hundred-year-old farms and former council houses to a small industrial yard. Ten years ago I co-led a CCT process for the village. It was called Discovery.

We were encouraged to walk our streets and look for signs of problems that needed addressing. Beyond some graffiti, rubbish and minor vandalism it was hard to spot poverty. Would the principles of God's vision, all God's people and our God apply here?

GOD'S VISION

Many churches in the UK have become increasingly involved in social action in the last twenty years. I think that this trend has been influenced by awareness of growing inequality, the influence of holistic or integral mission theology and the impact of highly visible initiatives such as food banks, Christians Against Poverty's debt counselling and Street Pastors.

Our church too has gone on a journey towards a broader vision. Sometimes the energy has come from theology and urgency. For instance, our pastor has helped us understand God's call to look after creation and how vital this is with the increasingly severe and frequent droughts, floods and hurricanes that bring death and misery to many.

We have now reached a stage where our church is helping each one of the four core relationships[2] to flourish. Initiatives have included:

---

[2] See Chapter 3.

- restoring a relationship with God through growing in our understanding of God's word through the Bible Project
- restoring relationships with others by providing practical and legal support to a community member suffering from addictive hoarding and coaching children who are struggling with school
- restoring a relationship with ourselves through contemplative prayer, retreats and worship
- restoring relationships with creation through Eco Church,[3] changing to environmentally friendly energy sources and cutting back on flights, car journeys and meat eating.

ALL GOD'S PEOPLE

We've increasingly realised how each of us has valuable things to contribute, such as Celia's delicious chocolate cakes for the community café. And we've seen that it's deeply helpful when we work with members of the wider community. So, for example, we've joined with other environmentally concerned villagers to challenge more and more villagers to switch their energy supplier.

And on a greater scale we will be supporting the district government in its measures to tackle climate change.

OUR GOD

All of this rests on the grace, transforming power and guidance of our loving Almighty God. Reverend Alan Jonas, our church vicar, explains:

> *Prayer underpins everything we do in the parish of Westcott. Morning prayer, prayer in services, prayer meetings, prayer through the day, times of focused prayer in response to particular situations, are the bedrock, vital to all that we do. A Christian who does not pray is like a beggar who inherited a fortune but continued to live in poverty because they could not be bothered to collect the inheritance.*
>
> *Our prayer is about growing ever deeper in relationship with God, who loves us through and through. We pray and listen for His wisdom, guidance and priorities; we pray that His kingdom will grow in our*

---

[3] An excellent initiative from A Rocha.

> *place, that lives will be blessed. We pray to be released from the power of sin, to be freed from all evil. We seek to come to God in complete openness of being – offering all that we are, our needs and desires, knowing that His grace will be sufficient for all of our needs. We seek to praise God and glorify Him and His kingdom.*
>
> *In short, we pray the 'Lord's Prayer'. Sometimes, we witness obvious miracles – healings of body, mind and spirit. We rejoice in such events but know they are 'signs' – pointing to the fullness of life there can/will be in Christ Jesus when His kingdom comes. More generally, we see the consequent blessings of being formed in prayer, in ever deeper relationships between the members of our church, in people coming to faith and growing in faith, in mission in Westcott and beyond.*
>
> *Prayer is essential, elemental to our lives individually and together as the church in Westcott.*

So those of us who live in the Minority World have the same calling as those who live in the Majority World: to work under God's leadership to help grow His kingdom. And we can apply the same core principles of God's vision, all God's people and our God to outwork this calling.

NOT-SO-WISE AND WISE COMPASSION
This approach and attitude can also result in a radically different way of relating to our sisters and brothers in the Majority World. Frankly, the way we relate often needs to change.

My friend Bob, a tall man with a Yorkshire accent, is part of St Luke's Church in a nearby city in the UK. It's vibrant, based on the Bible and committed to discipleship. But its approach to Christians in Bolivia was based on misunderstandings and 'not-so-wise' compassion.

St Luke's Church for many years provided financial support to an orphanage in Cochabamba in Bolivia. Members of the congregation had visited the orphanage, been moved by the vulnerability of the orphans and committed to give to improve their situation.

However, both parties in this relationship gradually became increasingly frustrated. St Luke's became worn down by frequent requests for funding and disappointed that the advice they gave was often not followed.

The Bolivians, in turn, struggled with the sense that St Luke's wanted to dictate from thousands of miles away without understanding the local context, and did not trust them to make wise decisions. The fact that St Luke's were providing money meant that there was a power imbalance.

Wherever we are located, local churches have a similar calling to work towards restoring the four key broken relationships, which in turn results in more of life in all its fullness. This is illustrated in the 'Life in all its fullness ecosystem' picture in Appendix 2.

The picture shows two trees (representing the church): the larger one for the Majority World and the smaller for the Minority World. The bees illustrate the opportunity we have to cross-pollinate each other's lives and work as we humbly learn from and pray for each other.

Sometimes churches that are more wealthy or have more formal education can assume they have most to give and little or nothing to receive. However, I have learned that people living in poverty often have much to teach, perhaps particularly in terms of deep faith and generous sharing of the little they have.

Relationships between churches in the Minority and Majority Worlds generally work best when there is no direct funding involved as money can easily skew relationships. Eventually St Luke's decided to switch their financial support to a CCT initiative in Cochabamba. This led to a much more equal relationship and more sustainable change.

Diane Holt, Director for Thrive Ireland, adds these reflections:

Poverty in the richer countries of the Minority World looks different and is often isolated in unseen pockets. And many of the local churches we work with are better-off ones where people do not have the experience of living in poverty. This can lead to much misunderstanding and judging of people. The poorer estates are actually very varied with many people who work extremely hard.

We need to understand that the poor are not poor people. We are all equally broken. And the poor are not helpless. Many Protestant churches here in Northern Ireland like life to be tidy but communities and relationships are messy.

There are also lots of similarities with the Majority World. I have learned so much from Majority World sisters and brothers, especially from Moses Kamau's work[4] in the slums in Nairobi.

Sadly, in the Minority World, the theology of the four broken relationships isn't getting through, perhaps because it's not taught at theological colleges. And also because there are not enough links between theology and practice. Most clergy leave their training totally unprepared to serve in contexts of social deprivation.

Churches often perceive that the gospel message is just about the need to be saved and so do not lobby about most social issues and injustice, often focusing on abortion and gay marriage. There is a serious disconnect between faith and much of real life.

A lot of Christians view God as a magician: thinking, I don't have to do anything. When in fact at the end of the day, it's you and me, God's people, carrying His presence within us, who need to do something to bring change.

And Christian international charities can be part of the problem if we see churches primarily as income sources rather than as groups who we could help mobilise to bring transformation in their own locality.

There are some good initiatives such as growing joint initiatives between the Evangelical Alliance, Christians Against Poverty, the Cinnamon Trust, the Trussell Trust and Thrive Ireland. I think that actually the wider communities often have more to offer the churches than the churches have to offer the wider communities. And when churches engage in relational ways with poorer communities it's so life-enhancing, we get the opportunity to see God at work.

You can find more thought-provoking and practical reflections from Diane on her Thrive Ireland blog.

---

[4] https://www.urbanimpactkenya.org/

So we know what vision we are aiming for and who is on the team. But the problems could still look daunting. We therefore now need to focus on our God Himself and how his character and power make impossible things possible.

EXPLORING FURTHER

- If you live in the Minority World, to what extent is your church involved in working with and serving the wider community? Which of the principles in this book could help your church catalyse transformation?
- If your church has relationships with local church(es) in another part of the world, to what extent are those relationships shaped by the power of funding? And how much are those relationships characterised by mutual learning, humility and prayer? What could be done to improve the connection?

OUR GOD

CHAPTER 10
AND IMAGINE IF …

Have you ever eaten a rat? Ormilla doesn't look like a 'rat eater'. She's a beautiful young lady with a shy smile and is dressed in a sunshine-yellow salwar kameez. She stands out a mile from the children who mill around her. Yet Ormilla and her community are known as 'rat eaters' and it's not meant as a compliment.

Ormilla is unfortunate enough to belong to the very lowest of this country's nine hundred sub-castes of 'untouchable' people. As a 'mahadalit' (meaning 'most crushed'), Ormilla's traditional place in life is to do the dirtiest jobs, to be banned from drinking water from wells used by higher castes and to be forced to eat separately at school. That's if she ever got to school.[1] Yet Ormilla is a remarkable lady and what has happened in her community challenges this story.

Ormilla used to have to go without food. *So I would drink water to fill my stomach as that was the only way to try to ease my hunger pains. But I wanted to study. I heard there was a church nearby and that if I went there they would guide me.* The church did help, using their own small resources to provide $12 for the entrance costs for school and supporting Ormilla for extra tuition. *Now I am in Standard 11 studying science, the only person in the entire history of my village to get this far.*

Ormilla believes she has been blessed and longs to pass on that blessing to the children around her. *I want every child to be able to study like me.* She is currently looking to begin a non-formal school in her community.

Later on I am playing a game with a lively group of kids in a nearby mahadalit community. It's a fun game called Samson, Delilah and the lion, and the kids are particularly enjoying roaring like lions at each other. Each precious child here is part of a non-formal school started by the church and community. They demonstrate to me their perfect knowledge of the English alphabet and, rather shyly, their beautiful singing. Life for them is beginning to look more hopeful.

---

[1] Only one in fifty mahadalit women can read and write.

There are many other signs of hope in this community. I walk past new brick houses being built – in all nineteen have sprung up in the last year. Encouraged by the dynamic local pastor, the community have lobbied the previously uninterested local government. As a result, sixty-two of the seventy-five families here have now gained access to the government benefits they are due.

We drove to the village along five hundred metres of new, government-funded road. The community has planted trees to help look after their land. Realising the problems that resulted from their previous involvement in brewing strong alcohol, the community have completely stopped.

THE THIRD PRINCIPLE

This story is another example of what can happen when ordinary local churches engage with the wonderful breadth of God's kingdom vision, working together as all God's people to use their own small resources to start to make that vision come true. That's two of this book's three fundamental principles for kingdom transformation.

The third and final principle is probably the most important. There's a substantial limit to what we can do as humans. As I've mentioned before, the feeding of the 5,000 did not fundamentally happen because the disciples picked up on Jesus' vision to also respond to the hunger of the crowd, helpful and important though that was.

The miracle also was not just about the young boy being willing to share his precious but seemingly deeply inadequate lunch, though that too was important. The core reason for the incredible events of that day was that Jesus was right at the centre with his compassion and divine power.

The type of deep transformation in South Asia described above is not limited to just a few communities. It has spread from just thirty communities in 2016 to over nine hundred in 2021, across half of the country. Such incredible growth has only been possible because of God's gracious response to the prayers of the godly people who lead this work and an ongoing outpouring of His Spirit in miracles.

Churches and communities have blossomed as God has protected people from poisonous snake bites, healed a woman from severe bleeding when she just came into earshot of Christian worship, fed seventy people from rice and fish that was only enough for six people and raised a boy from the dead!

We need to put our trust in God because only God can do miracles in people's hearts, do the seemingly impossible and bring national and global-scale change.

GOD CHANGES HEARTS

Sometimes I think that we work as if we could achieve all our goals with the right vision, plans and finances. And yet as I reflect on the Bible I come to the humbling conclusion that we can't do what is most necessary: change another person's heart.

The Bible seems to say that only two people can profoundly change a human heart. One is the person themselves, for example as 'Pharaoh hardened his heart' in Exodus 8:15 and 32. The other is God: 'the LORD hardened Pharaoh's heart' in Exodus 11:10. These verses don't mention other well-meaning locals or outsiders.

But for deep change to come we need people's hearts to move. So that they become more humble, generous, inclusive, hopeful, faithful. We need to realise that we are totally reliant on God who alone can 'give you a new heart and put a new spirit in you; I will remove from you your heart of stone and give you a heart of flesh' (Ezek. 36:26).

GOD DOES THE SEEMINGLY IMPOSSIBLE IN RESPONSE TO PRAYER

I wonder whether you, like me, need the truths in His word and the stories of how he has acted powerfully in *our* times as a reminder of how great God's power is.

Personally I am encouraged by an experience I had in the Democratic Republic of Congo (DRC) in 2008.

I found it hard to fully relax the first time I travelled in the DRC. The streets of Bukavu were full of brightly dressed women buying and selling, but every time I looked at the surrounding hills I felt unsafe. Rebel militias could strike at any time.

One warlord in particular stood out. General Nkunda had an eagle- topped cane and a brutal reputation. His militia were highly effective fighters and so, when he threatened to march on the capital Kinshasa and take over the government, it was no idle threat.

But, in his pride, he had forgotten that 'the Most High is sovereign over the kingdoms of men and gives them to whoever he wishes' (Dan. 4:17).

And he had forgotten that our God responds to the prayers of His ordinary people. Some of us decided it was time to pray that God would humble General Nkunda. We chose to trust in the truth of this verse in Daniel. So across the world there were prayers – in DRC, in Tearfund's Wednesday prayer meeting and in my small village church. It was one of the biggest-scale prayers I had ever prayed and seemed almost too big to ask for.

However, God answered us. Soon after we prayed, General Nkunda's militia split in two, thus halving his power. A few weeks after that, on 22 January 2009, he was arrested in Rwanda and has been under house arrest ever since, indicted for war crimes and crimes against humanity. Our God is much bigger than the issues we face.

So will you and I pray big? Will we ask for major changes in our world from our God 'who is able to do immeasurably more than all we ask or imagine' (Eph. 3:20)? It's not the size of our faith that matters but the size of our God in whom we have faith.

GOD BRINGS NATIONAL AND GLOBAL CHANGE WHEN WE PRAY

In my seventeen years working for Tearfund there is one prayer time that particularly stands out, both for the sense of God's presence and the scale of the impact.

It was a warm evening in Kenya in April 2011 when I felt called to repent on behalf of the UK. Tears flowed down my cheeks as I considered how far the UK has wandered from God's ways. I was in good company, for around the room people, including many bishops, from fifteen nations were similarly on their knees. I believe God meant it when he said:'If my people, who are called by my name, will humble themselves and pray and seek my face and turn from their wicked ways, then I will hear from heaven, and I will forgive their sin and will heal their land' (2 Chr. 7:14).

Does your nation need healing? Mine certainly does. Shockingly, a quarter of women in the UK will experience domestic violence in their lifetime. The Trussell Trust provided 1.2 million emergency food supplies to people in the UK last year; of these, 436,000 were to children. Over half of the people in the UK now say they have no faith.

Does God answer such big prayers? I've seen plenty of evidence that He does. For example, the bloodless fall of the Berlin Wall on 9

November 1989 was directly linked to years of prayers for peace and peaceful demonstrations starting from St Nicholas, one ordinary church.[2] Similar prayer movements contributed to the peaceful end of apartheid in South Africa, when most commentators expected major bloodshed. And the results of the prayer meeting I was at in Kenya? They continue to reverberate around the world to this day as God releases hundreds of thousands of people from poverty.

If. If is the key word. Will you and your church humble yourselves and pray for your nation? The results could be awesome.

WHAT COULD YOU DO?
So in this book I have tried to show how, through putting into practice three comparatively simple principles, we can work with God to produce deep, broad and long-lasting transformation.

Those vital principles are to:

- grasp the wonderful breadth of God's kingdom vision of restored relationships with God, others, ourselves and creation
- work humbly with all God's people using the modest resources we have
- pray and rely deeply on our God and His amazing power and grace.

May God grant you inspiration and wisdom as you consider how to respond to the ideas in this book. May each person you know flourish and experience more of the fullness of life that Jesus brings. And may He multiply the works of your hands beyond all you could ask or imagine.

EXPLORING FURTHER

- Insight: As you reflect on this book, what are the main points that you think are important to remember and work on?
- Intention: What step(s) would you like to take to help bring deeper transformation in your church, community and nation?

---

[2] Peter Crutchley, 'Did a prayer meeting really bring down the Berlin Wall and end the Cold War?', BBC Religion and Ethics, 9 October 2015: https://dq5pwpg1q8ru0.cloudfront.net/2020/10/30/08/22/09/91c735a7-e75b-4384-8f2f-68076f71fbd6/Fall%20of%20Berlin%20Wall.pdf

- Often it's valuable to see things in practice. This can help us to know what is possible and to learn from strong examples. So you may find it helpful to contact the Tearfund office in your country[3] to ask if they can tell you where to visit to see CCT in action.

---

[3] You can contact Tearfund offices directly or through:
https://www.tearfund.org/useful-links/contact-us

PRINCIPLES

Tearfund understands that CCT is bounded by six principles which connect with the three principles in this book as follows:

Principle in this book	Tearfund CCT principle
God's vision	1) driven by biblical theology of integral mission and dependence on God
	2) intentionally seeks the restoration of all four broken relationships
	4) mobilises the church to become an agent of holistic change in the community
All God's people	3) facilitates Bible reflection to bring about mindset, values and behaviour change
	5) relies on inclusive, participatory processes to bring about ownership and sustainable change
	6) celebrates and mobilises local resources, increases agency and releases community potential
Our God	1) driven by biblical theology of integral mission and dependence on God

LIFE IN ALL ITS FULLNESS 'ECOSYSTEM'

LIFE IN ALL ITS FULLNESS EXPLAINED

GOD THE 'HEAD GARDENER'	God is the 'Head Gardener' and needs to be at the centre of all our thinking and practice. 'If a person remains in me and me in them, they will bear much fruit, apart from me you can do nothing' John 15v5
FRUIT: LIFE IN ALL ITS FULLNESS	Our aim is that people living in poverty experience 'Life in all its fullness' John 10v10 (or in development language 'holistic transformation')
TREE: CHURCH IN ALL ITS FORMS	God's main agent for change is His church and this varies in form according to context. In most contexts the church is present 'above ground' but in some it is not present or visibly present. In such locations the expression of God's church tend to be Christians working in operational teams or Christian partners.
FERTILE SOIL: MOBILISED CHURCH AND COMMUNITY	Evidence shows that mobilised churches and communities provide fertile soil for transformation. This mobilisation will be contextually specific: in some locations 'church and community transformation', in some 'church mobilisation' and in some 'community mobilisation'.
BRANCHES: TECHNICAL COMPETENCES, INCUBATION AREAS, LINKS TO GOVERNMENT AND BUSINESS	As churches and communities work towards life in all its fullness they will be able to bring considerable amounts of change using their own resources and skills. However there are limits to their ability and resources so there is a need for technical support, effective links to government and business. Assistant Gardeners can either directly provide these or help network them in.
ROOTS: WHOLE LIFE DISCIPLESHIP (FOLLOWING JESUS)	Deep and strong roots are essential for effective transformation (Mark 4v6). It is 'transformed people who bring transformation' Michel Kayitba, Moucecore. The more that God's people are transformed the more they will be able to live generously, forgive radically, serve the most marginalised etc. Deep discipleship roots also enable God's people to survive the pressures of persecution, false theologies such as Prosperity Gospel and false worldviews such as materialism.
GROUNDWATER: 'WHOLE LIFE THEOLOGY AND ECCLESIOLOGY'	Whole Life Discipleship draws its life from: whole life (kingdom/ integral) God thinking (theology) and church thinking (ecclesiology).
RAIN: PRAYER	A tree's life ultimately depends on rain. In the same way, life in all its fullness is only possible through God who is the source and very definition of life (Deut 30v20 and John 14v6). Prayer, in various forms, is essential for the heart transformation (Ezekiel 36v26), holistic change and scale of change required. Only God can do 'immeasurably more than all we ask or imagine' Ephesians 3v20.
ASSISTANT GARDENERS:	INGOs such as Tearfund, national partners and Inspired Individuals are assistant gardeners working under God's leadership to help the church in all its forms bring life in all its fullness. This requires working with others on whatever parts of the ecosystem require attention in a given context.
BEES: CROSS POLLINATION	God's people in the Global South and Global North need to work together as parts of the body of Christ (Ephesians 4v15f6) to see life in all its fullness come more fully. This involves mutual prayer support, crosslearning and resource transfer.
WIND: HAZARDS	Any community is subject to hazards including both natural and humanmade disasters so a core role for churches and communities with INGO/ NGO support is increasing resilience and, where appropriate, effective disaster response
FOREST: DENOMINATIONS AND CHURCH NETWORKS	The Assistant Gardeners have the resources to support comparatively small scale transformation (ie effectively pilot or example communities). Church denominations and church networks however have the reach to take these ideas and spread them at national, regional and global scales. Ultimately this scale up needs to be resourced by their own resources.
LARGER TREE: GLOBAL SOUTH	The larger tree represents a community in the Global South, otherwise known as the 'Majority World' (ie where the majority of the world's population live).
SMALLER TREE: GLOBAL NORTH	The smaller tree represents a community in the Global North otherwise known as the 'Minority World' (ie where a minority of the world's population live). Churches here have a similar mandate from God to work towards life in all its fullness (or God's kingdom) in their communities.
RULER: DESIGN, MONITORING, EVALUATION, ACCOUNTABILITY AND LEARNING	INGOs such as Tearfund need to use Design, Monitoring, Evaluation, Accountability and Learning' (DMEAL) approaches to understand and improve the effectiveness of the work they support or do.

ACKNOWLEDGEMENTS

I am very grateful to:

God who graciously rescued me, has loved me faithfully and allowed me to walk with Him and His people as He brings deep transformation, hope and joy.

Church and community members who have welcomed, taught and inspired me and graciously responded to the hundreds of questions from this enthusiastic guest!

To Romnal Colas, Anne Mumbi, Rei Crizaldo, Bishop Anthony Poggo, Brian Fikkert, Levourne Passiri, Florence Muindi and Diane Holt who contributed valuable insights for this book and other fellow travelers and friends in Tearfund, Emmanuel International, Friends of Umoja and my local church.

Sheryl Hall for her enthusiastic introduction to Regnum books, Paul Bendor-Samuel for your encouraging response and to Tony Gray and Elizabete Santos for your invaluable design and practical work. Stephanie Heald for two hours of insightful advice at Heathrow airport.

Jonathan Mayo, Jenny Flanaggan, Rachel Musk and Mark Galpin, as more experienced writers, for your encouragement, ideas and careful proofreading.

Lastly, and certainly not least, to my dear family, friends and prayer companions whose love, interest and support makes my heart sing.

BV - #0058 - 311022 - C0 - 210/148/4 - PB - 9781914454530 - Gloss Lamination